IMAGES OF ENGLAND

NEWCASTLE EAST END

IMAGES OF ENGLAND

NEWCASTLE EAST END

RAY MARSHALL AND THE
NEWCASTLE EVENING CHRONICLE

TEMPUS

Frontispiece: Osborne Road, Jesmond, 1956. The new lampposts mark out the Lord Mayor of Newcastle's (Alderman A.C. Curly) residence, although the car may not look apt for civic duty.

First published 2005

Tempus Publishing Limited
The Mill, Brimscombe Port,
Stroud, Gloucestershire, GL5 2QG
www.tempus-publishing.com

British Library Cataloguing in Publication Data.
A catalogue record for this book is available from the British Library.

ISBN 0 7524 3629 5

Typesetting and origination by Tempus Publishing Limited.
Printed in Great Britain.

Contents

Osborne Road, Jesmond, 1960. A panoramic view of Newcastle taken from the steeple of St George's Church, Jesmond, shows Osborne Road leading down into the 'big smoke'.

Introduction

As heavy industry began to flourish on the River Tyne, it was to the east of Newcastle that the new 'Captains of Industry' decided to enjoy the spoils of their labour and build their new palaces. What later became Jesmond, Heaton, Benton and Walker were deep denes and forests, potted with small hamlets and villages. This rural setting provided a restful environment for the workaholic entrepreneurs of the eighteenth and nineteenth centuries. But times were changing fast and land was in demand, especially in an area with such good links to the coast, the river and the region's main business centre, Newcastle. The march of progress had begun; the denes were filled in and the forests cleared as industry moved in. New factories were soon springing up to supply the fledgling shipyards on the river. A series of small coal mines had up until this time provided the main employment, but these were swept away as heavy industry moved in to take their place. Orders were arriving regularly for new ships as the reputation of Tyneside shipbuilders spread throughout the world and, as keels were laid, the supply and support industries mushroomed. At the same time the suburbs of Newcastle were bursting the city boundaries and housing spread into the new areas following in the wake of industry. In 1867 an amalgamation between the Emperor of Elswick, Lord Armstrong, and shipbuilder Charles Mitchell, who had the Low Walker yard, created a whole new reservoir of knowledge and skill in the industry to take it on to a new and higher level. Shipbuilding wasn't the only place were reputations were being made. Alongside Lord Armstrong and Charles Mitchell came Charles Parsons, who had been apprenticed at Lord Armstrong's Elsick works. Parsons believed the steam engine was basically inefficient and in 1884 invented the steam turbo-generator. It may have been only seven kilowatts, but it was a start. Four years later he started up his own factory in Heaton and it was in 1897 that the *Turbinia*, driven by Parsons' own steam turbine engine, took the world by storm and changed shipping forever. In the ensuing years his workforce developed the skills not only to drive ships but also to create transformers to keep the world's power stations running. Parsons' steam turbine and its associated generator had become the foundation stone of modern electrical power supply and it is said that every time you switch on a light in your home you are benefiting from the work of Sir Charles Parsons. But it was not just heavy industry and coal which was bringing fame to Tyneside; the area was also famous for the manufacture of glass and ropes and another firm was gaining a world-wide reputation – Maling pottery. Maling pottery was first produced in Sunderland from 1762 but the factory was moved to the Ouseburn area of Newcastle in 1817 by Robert Maling, a third-generation family member to be involved in the business. At this time the firm had not developed its world-wide reputation and its output was only competing with other local firms. Robert's son, Christopher Thompson Maling, changed all that. He took over the business in the 1850s and took it in a new direction. He had found a way of mass-producing packaging containers with machinery, instead of making it by hand. As well as pottery, the firm turned out jars for meat paste, ointment, printing ink and marmalade. According to records, Keiller's of Dundee ordered as many as 1,500,000 jars in one year. Maling opened a second pottery in 1859 which could output as much in one week as the Ouseburn Bridge pottery could produce in a year. A third pottery opened in 1879 which claimed to be the biggest pottery in the world – and it dwarfed its predecessor. The smaller pottery closed in the 1920s after the General Strike affected its coal supplies. In 1929 Maling joined forces with another big East End firm, Ringtons, who sold tea door-to-door and produced what was basically an advertising 'gimmick' – selling the tea packaged in a caddy produced by Maling. The association with Rington tea lasted until 1962 when increasing competition forced Maling out of business. They lost a contract to supply crockery to the London & North Eastern Railway Co. to a Japanese company who undercut their price by 75 per cent. The factory finally closed in 1963. Most of these heavy industries have now gone, given way to the march of progress and centralisation. The East End of Newcastle is now a popular residential area flourishing with small industries and shops, ready to enjoy the challenges of the twenty-first century.

one

Jesmond

The name Jesmond probably means 'mouth of the Ouseburn', although many prefer the more romantic 'Jesus mound'. The area of Jesmond was given to Nicholas Grenville by Henry I in the twelfth century. Grenville's family built the first manor house in the district and also the famous shrine, St Mary's Chapel, which attracted pilgrims from all over the country. From around 1820 Jesmond emerged from being mainly an agricultural area, with several small coal mines, to become a place of residence for such men as G.W. Armstrong, Charles Mark Palmer, Henry F. Swan, G.B. Hunter and Charles Mitchell, who built mansions such as Jesmond Dene House and Jesmond Towers. Jesmond gradually became a suburb of its big neighbour, Newcastle, to which it was officially added in 1835. As a parish it had always been a part of St Andrew's in Newgate Street, Newcastle, until the Jesmond Parish Church was opened in 1861. Initially Jesmond had comprised of three small villages, Brandling, Jesmond Vale (built for industrial and mine workers) and Jesmond. From the 1870s these villages were enveloped in the suburban sprawl of housing spreading out from Newcastle and, eventually, from around 1880, Jesmond became the home of several top schools: Church High School, which opened in 1885, followed by Central High School, which moved to Eskdale Terrace in 1900. In 1906 the Royal Grammar School and La Sagesse High School both moved to the area. As Jesmond grew it developed a small transport system of its own when a horse-drawn tram came up Osborne Road. By 1880 the tram came to Mistletoe Road and in 1901 this was replaced by electric trams which later reached as far as Jesmond Avenue. From 1904 Jesmond had an electric train service, which has its echoes in today's Metro system.

Osborne Road, 1912. An electric tram and a car pass each other along the open sweep of a heavily tree-lined Osborne Road in Jesmond, Newcastle.

Above: Jesmond, 1903.
These flag-waving
youngsters are celebrating
Empire Day. This picture
was taken by an early
pioneer of photography,
Charles Mitford, who was
also Vicar of Mitford.

Right: Jesmond Dene,
1908. It's nearly all caps
and hats as a group of
young men and women
pose in a floral setting
after spending the day at
Jesmond Dene House.

Jesmond, 1951. Proof that steeplejacks had to have nerves of steel. The picture shows a steeplejack busy working on St George's Church.

Above: St George's Church, 1924. This church was designed by T.R. Spence and consecrated in 1888. Shipbuilder Charles Mitchell paid for the church to be built on the southern edge of his Jesmond Towers Estate.

Right: Jesmond Parish Church, 1931. The Union Jack flag flies proudly over the church on a cold January day.

Left: Holy Trinity Memorial Church, 1922. When this picture was taken it was the newest church in Newcastle. It was opened by the Bishop of Newcastle in September of that year with naval and military detachments present.

Below: Holy Trinity Church, 1936. The congregation listen to the sermon inside the church.

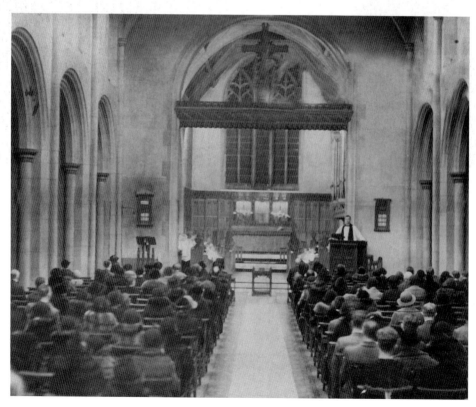

Jesmond Methodist Church, 1936. Parishioners gather for a special morning service.

Above: St George's Presbyterian Church, Jesmond Road, 1936. The church was due to become headquarters for the Home Teaching Society for the Blind.

Left: Jesmond Baptist Church, 1930.

Opposite, below: Joseph Willis outside his shop in Shieldfield Street, Shieldfield. Both of the pictures on this page were supplied by Joseph's grandson, Joe Miller, who says that the little girl holding her grandfather's hand is his mother, Dorothy Willis. Apparently Joe Willis died as a result of a mustard gas attack in the First World War.

Jesmond Dene, 1912. The cyclists above are from Jesmond Dene Cycle Club and include Joseph Willis, third from the right.

A load of splashing good fun for youngsters on a hot June day in 1963 at Brandling Park.

Families throng the paddling pool at Brandling Park on a sweltering August day in 1955.

Brandling Park, 1964. Boys will be boys, as they make life hard for the girls in the pool.

Earlier, in 1953, however, Brandling Park seems a much quieter and sedate pace for the young mums and their children.

Left: Jesmond Station, 1955. An *Evening Chronicle* reader wrote in to the local paper to say that the stationmaster and his staff were to be admired for the way they had beautified the platforms with flowerbeds. He went on to say it was a real pleasure for passengers when waiting for a train or when passing on the road above.

Below: Jesmond Station, 1948. Competing with thirty-two other stations in the region, the suburban station's platform gardens won a British Rail first prize.

Above: A Newcastle Corporation single-deck tramcar about to journey from Central Station in Newcastle to Osborne Road, Jesmond, in 1901.

Right: A Newcastle Corporation Blue Bus heads down from Gosforth en route to Newcastle Central Station in 1931. On its journey it will visit Market Street, Grey Street and St Nicholas's Cathedral.

Jesmond Baths, 1938. A workman passes by Jesmond Swimming Baths.

A clean-looking Jesmond Street with a lack of shoppers.

The beautiful interior of the Playhouse Theatre, pictured in 1936.

Crag Hall, 1931. Described as a pleasant old hall in Jesmond, with its shrub-lined paths and lawn, under which two old barrows (two-wheeled handcarts) were found in 1844.

Windsor Crescent pictured in quieter times, 1948.

The same street pictured in 1964, showing the gardens which are about to become a car park, according to a story in the *Evening Chronicle*.

Jesmond Road, 1967. A seemingly quiet road which is a far cry from the congested road of today.

Jesmond Road, 1961. Here we can see Siesta Houses, once occupied by Chapman's furniture shop, as well as the junction of Jesmond Road and the Great North Road before the construction of the central motorway through Newcastle.

Above and below: Jesmond Towers, 1931. Children line up outside the late Georgian house (which has had substantial Victorian additions) and is now La Sagesse High School. When these pictures were taken it had been leased to Osborne Grammar School. A John Dobson-designed building, it was originally named West Jesmond House until it was bought and renamed Jesmond Towers by shipbuilder Charles Mitchell, partner of Lord Armstrong. He enlarged it and his family lived there until the 1920s, after which it became a school.

STOTES HALL, NEWCASTLE-UPON-TYNE.

Above and right: Stotes Hall, 1946. This ancient house which stood on the east side of Jesmond Road was demolished around 1953. Above the entrance, pictured right, you can see the coat of arms of the Merchant Adventurers, dated 1607. It is thought to have been the first fortified manor in Northumberland to be constructed outside the city walls. Sir Richard Stote initially bought a house on the land in 1658 and it was given the name Stotes Hall. The Stotes Hall in the picture above may not have been the original one, but after many owners it was bought by Miss Doris Cowper in 1927 and renovated. It had also been used as a headquarters by St John's Ambulance Brigade.

Above, below and opposite: Jesmond banqueting hall, 1970. When Lord Armstrong found that his previous home in Jesmond Dene was not suitable for royal visitors, he had the banqueting hall built in 1862. John Dobson was the architect of the new building, which included a water-driven organ using pressure from Paddy Freeman's lake (a fall of about 15m). Both ends of the main hall had large arched windows and Dobson had it decorated with paintings and Greek statues in the alcoves. The oak table on which the meals were served would be moved aside for dancing. The lodge and the gatehouse, still in use today, were added around 1870. The banqueting hall lost its roof in a storm in the mid-1970s and the City Council refused to make the necessary repairs; it is now open to the elements, as shown in the pictures on the facing page. Now a Grade-II listed building, it has lately been used as a storage area for local stonemasons. Before the banqueting hall was built it had been the site of the Apple Tree Inn, which was relocated to Jesmond Grove.

Armstrong Bridge, April 1926. A tranquil scene, but the warning signs are up diverting heavy traffic to the steep gradient on the right.

Armstrong Bridge, April 1928. The signs have changed at the end of the bridge (which is now a tram stop). Two girls stand in the roadway, possibly waiting for the next tram?

Armstrong Bridge, 1983. Business is slow, but Chrissie and Janice are just testing the market on a Sunday morning before their business, Ripping Yarns, gets a national lift-off.

Armstrong Bridge, 1980. The famous open-air picture gallery is threatened with closure by Newcastle City Council's environmental health department, which faced a backlash from artists, visitors and a former Lord Mayor, Councillor Arthur Grey, who called the move ridiculous.

Armstrong Bridge, 1981. The bridge, designed and constructed in 1878 by W.G. Armstrong & Co., gives a superb view of Jesmond Dene. The bridge, linking Heaton and Jesmond, was pedestrianised in 1960 and is now the setting for a popular Sunday arts and crafts market.

Armstrong Bridge, 1963. Police guide vehicles away from the bridge which now seems to be set for one way traffic. A sign warns that a speed limit of 12mph is in force.

Above and below: Jesmond Dene, 1963. They may not be lions or tigers, but young visitors still flocked to Pet's Corner in the Dene to watch the rabbits at play.

Above and below: St Mary's Chapel, 1931. The picturesque ruins of St Mary's Chapel in Jesmond *(above)* and *(below)* as they appear in a painting by Robert Mills of Fenham North Lodge in 1821.

This historic park and garden was the gift
of
SIR WILLIAM GEORGE ARMSTRONG
(LORD ARMSTRONG)
in 1883 to the citizens of Newcastle as
an area of outstanding natural beauty

The Friends of Jesmond Dene
June 1999

Lord Armstrong (above right) had bought up most of what is now Jesmond Dene by 1862 and, with his wife planning the landscaping, turned what was described as a wilderness into a beautiful park. They rebuilt the riverbanks and introduced bridges, stepping stones and pathways. Under Lady Armstrong's guidance the river was split into a series of weirs and waterfalls to stunning effect. Armstrong gifted Jesmond Dene to the citizens of Newcastle in 1883.

Jesmond Dene, 1948. Sometimes known as the 'eye bridge', it proved useful to young ladies as a mirror as they pause on their walk through the Dene on a sunny day.

Jesmond Dene Mill, 1937. The ladders go up as repairs are carried out on the beautiful old mill.

This page and the next three photographs: A stunning series of pictures of Jesmond Dene. Here, a snow-covered Dene in 1965.

The snow may have gone in 1972, but it is still a Christmas card scene in the Dene.

Stepping stones in the Dene in 1946.

Above: Waterfalls on an autumn day in the Dene in1935.

Left: Jesmond Dene, 1956. Smoke comes from the roof of the old mill in Jesmond Dene.

Opposite, below: Jesmond Dene, 1928. Few cities in Britain could offer such an enchanting view.

Jesmond Dene, 1927. The old home of Paddy Freeman which had been in existence for 200 years before it had to make way for the expansion of city dwellings. Paddy (Patrick) Freeman and his family took over the house after moving from Windmill Hills in Gateshead around 1795 to farm and mill in High Heaton, but the family moved away following Sir William Armstrong's enclosure of Jesmond Dene in 1862.

Above: Jesmond Dene, 1939. Water-less falls: the stream has been diverted for spring-cleaning.

Left: The Princess Mary Hospital. This was originally the Northern Counties Orphanage and was paid for by prominent local families the Abbotts and the Phillipsons. It continued to be used as such until the outbreak of the Second World War when it was taken over by the Princess Mary Maternity Hospital which moved there from Jubilee Road.

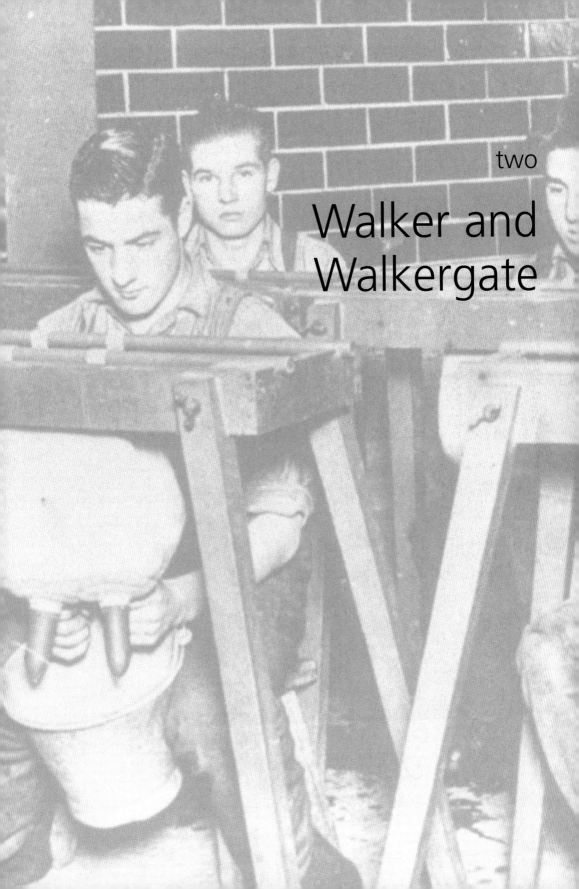

two

Walker and Walkergate

It is believed that the name Walker comes from Wall-Car, which means the marsh by the wall, referring to the Roman wall which ran along what today is known as the Fossway, leading to Wallsend. Until the middle of the eighteenth century, Walker was an agricultural area with large areas of deep denes covered by dense woodland running down to the River Tyne. Newcastle Corporation bought the land in 1715 and filled the denes in with ballast, which allowed factories and shipyards to be built. There were ten pits in the Walker area which led to the establishment of the chemical industry, mainly because of the Salt Springs in the King Pit. William Losh eventually closed his alkali works at Scotswood to set up Walker Alkali Works – manufacturing sulphuric acid, copperas, caustic soda and dyes – by the river to exploit the natural resource here that his factory needed. He also built the Walker West School for the workers' children. Along with Thomas Bell and Thomas Wilson, Losh opened an engineering works and an iron foundry in Walker where he manufactured rails for the first railway, steam engines for collieries and mills, and iron boilers for ship plates. The closeness to the sea of the ironworks also meant that Walker was an ideal place for shipbuilding and John Coutts set up a shipyard at Low Walker, which was later sold on to J. Wigham Richardson in 1860. This became the Neptune Shipbuilding & Engineering Works of Wigham Richardson & Co. Ltd. Charles Mitchell began his shipbuilding works in Walker in 1852 and later amalgamated with Sir W.G. Armstrong to become Armstrong Mitchell & Co. Ltd. They then merged with Whitworth to become Armstrong Whitworth and opened the Walker Naval Yard in 1912 on the site of the old ironworks. The rising cost of importing raw materials had forced the ironworks to close in 1891 when production was transferred to Teesside. The chemical industry soon followed south to Middlesbrough, to later become ICI. Walker became part of Newcastle in 1904, which resulted in a rapid development of housing. In 1920 the estate of Walkerdene was built and in 1930 building started on a large council estate in central and southern Walker. This was preceded by a large slum-clearance programme.

Walker Quay, 1847. A Carmichael drawing of the Tyne 160 years ago.

Name that place. Clue number one: it's in Walker. Clue number two: it's a pub and this was how it looked nearly 150 years ago. If it still has you beaten it's not surprising, for the Scrogg Inn has changed almost beyond recognition. The pub, in Scrogg Road, near the corner of Welbeck Road, at one time stood alone in fields. Now the area has been built-up and the original building has been added to. This watercolour painted in 1923, which may be a copy of an original, was found amongst a pile of rubbish.

Walker Naval Yard in 1980. The berths lie empty and the cranes stand idle.

Walker, 1961. Only a couple of years before this picture was taken Walker was an area choked with ageing houses, broken-down garages, rubbish heaps and allotments. This picture shows how all this has been swept away as part of a rebuilding programme to bring housing in the area up to date with flats and spacious housing estates.

Above and right: Walker Park, 1956. When repairs were due to the Robbie Burns statue in Walker Park, Newcastle, it was suggested it was turned around to face 'the heath and heather, rills and hills of Bonnie Scotland'. However the suggestion was not taken up.

Walker Training Farm, 1929. Because of mass unemployment; thousands were retrained for other jobs, such as the young men in this photograph who are undertaking milking lessons in preparation for farm work.

Church Street, 1960. The changing face of Walker, with housing disappearing to make way for new modern developments.

Walker Road, 1961. Three miles of Walker Road wound through some of Newcastle's heaviest industry and, although you would not guess from the picture above, residents still complained about the volume of traffic.

This horse-drawn ambulance, belonging to Walkergate Hospital in 1922, was a familiar sight around Walker for many years.

Church Street. Trolleybus No. 599, the last to be used in service in Newcastle. Taken shortly before the street was closed to traffic, this picture shows the bus pulling across the junction with Proctor Street.

three

Shieldfield

Shieldfield is first listed in 1260 as Selingfield as one of the townships controlled by Nicholas of Byker. According to local records, the local militia mustered at Shellfelde in 1544 before embarking at Tynemouth and sailing to Scotland. Over the years Shieldfield has been referred to in references as Shelewood, Shelefold and Shelesfield. In Anglo-Saxon times the word Shieldfield seems to have meant shelter in the forest clearing. Shiel, Shield or Sheele can be translated as shelter and field means a patch of felled or cleared land in a forest area. The area always seems to have been used as a public parkland. In the 1600s horse racing in the area was well-supported. Maps from the early 1700s show that the area was largely rural with very few houses and separated from Newcastle by the deep valley of Pandon Burn. When Shieldfield was enclosed in 1738 angry locals used horses to trample down hedges and private owners responded by advertising in the *Newcastle Courant* that trespassers would be prosecuted. But by 1800 the urban spread was beginning to arrive and Shieldfield became a popular retreat for Tyneside's businessmen. George Armstrong was born there in 1810. A new bridge was built above Pandon Burn, opening the way to North Shields in 1812 and linking the area with Newcastle. Sandyford also took advantage of the new bridge with an influx of new housing and tenants. Sandyford Lane was renamed Sandyford Road in 1878 and was soon extended to Lambert's Leap and included Benton Lane up to the junction with Jesmond Road. By 1890 there was strong pressure for more housing in the area and it was decided that some of the mansions and their large grounds would be acquired for development. In 1892, following the death of brewer J.S. Arnison, Sandyford House was demolished and the burn infilled, which allowed housing to expand rapidly. In 1899 the Goldspink Hall Estate was bought up and the ten-acre site was covered with housing. In the same year R.G. Hoare died, at Jesmond Park. The north end of Cradlewell was developed from 1904 to 1907 and the streets were all named after cabinet ministers. The 1960s brought major redevelopment and motorway construction to Sandyford, an area that once boasted many stately homes, of which now only Villa Real remains.

Left: Pandon Dene: the Dene as it appeared more than 170 years ago, *c.* 1831. The valley was eventually filled in and a new bridge erected, hence the name New Bridge Street.

Opposite, below: Hopping bound, 1913. Long gone are the days when you could see an elephant pulling a van along the road towards Newcastle – followed by two camels. Well, plenty of folk around these parts used to see such fascinating traffic scenes when our roads were less noisy and frenetic – but much more colourful. This photograph was taken on the last mile or two from the city boundaries on the way to the Hoppings at Jesmond Vale.

Above: Jesmond Vale, 1914. The sound of the Gavioli organ is in the air; there's the noise of the steam tractors, steadily chuffing away as they rock on their wheels, powering the side-shows; the smell of fish and chips and the sound of people laughing and shouting. It's the Hoppings, of course. But wait a minute, it's not on Newcastle Town Moor … did you know that the Hoppings were once held in Jesmond Vale? And here's the picture to prove it. It's the summer of 1914 and the local troops are busy exercising on Town Moor ready for the war that is looming a few months away. This picture was taken from Armstrong Bridge, where the photographer focused his cumbersome paraphernalia and registered the scene for posterity. There isn't a motor vehicle to be seen down on the ground of what in those days was called Green Pool. As a matter of fact, there are only two steam tractors to be seen, but there are lots of caravans, with the horse shafts let down in front of them. The horses are out grazing somewhere. The roundabouts are powered by steam and a plume of smoke hangs over them.

Copland Terrace, 1957. Two young girls head their separate ways and, if you look closely, there are a number of shops amongst the terraced houses.

Copland Terrace, 1957. A public health inspector came under fire for 'overdoing' the list of defects to property in Shieldfield and Copland Terrace.

Sallyport Crescent, 1953. A car rumbles down the cobbled crescent, heading toward the Quayside.

Market Street, 1961. Shieldfield flats rise up in the background, and on the left is a new BBC building surmounted by the mast and reflector which receives outside broadcasts.

Kent Street, 1958. Children at play in a Shieldfield back lane. The state of the area may make you wonder what dangers lay in wait for these youngsters amongst the grime and the rubble.

Henry Street, 1960. Although nearly derelict, people still lived in this gas–lit street.

Nixon Street, 1961. Homes which were earmarked to be demolished.

Kensington Terrace, 1958. Obviously a wealthy area, judging by the number of cars parked outside the homes of residents.

Angle Terrace, Rosehill, 1929. The girl in the picture is the daughter of John Cassidy, who took over the Dobson's market garden.

Stephenson Road, 1963. A small branch of the Trustees Savings Bank is tucked away amongst the shops. The lack of parking restrictions made it a safe haven for drivers.

Opposite, above: Kirsop Street, 1957. If it wasn't for the small signs you would never have thought the street contained a shop.

Opposite, below: Garden Street, 1961. Garden Street was classed as one of Newcastle's worst slum areas.

Shieldfield, 1950. A mechanical snow-loader, capable of moving seven tons of snow in five minutes, is at work. It was the first made in Britain and was undergoing tests. Unfortunately the sun came out and everything turned to slush.

King Charles House, 1959. King Charles I was brought to Newcastle after surrendering to the Scots in 1646 at Newark. During his imprisonment at Anderson House he was allowed to travel to Shieldfield to play his favourite sport, golf. It was recorded that during these excursions he would use this house to rest.

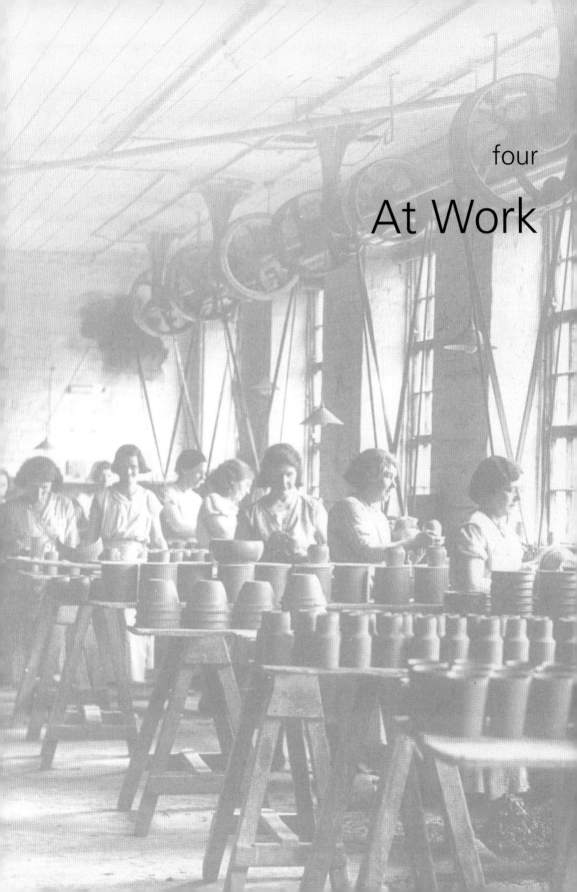

four

At Work

There has never been any doubting of the skill and willingness of the Geordie worker, but in these days of call centres and franchise businesses there is not much room for the skilled craftsman of yesterday. Men from Parsons would build generators to service the power supply of many of the world's major cities. Specialists from Parsons would travel the world checking and balancing turbine engines so that they ran more effectively. The skill of workers at such places as Maling pottery will live on through the collectors' items they produced in abundance. But small businesses have also fallen by the wayside. Take a look at wheelwright Ron Green at work (page 66). An essential trade before the Second World War, the 1950s and '60s saw the need for such wagon wheels decline until they were only required for agricultural shows and museums. Let's not forget too the telephone exchange girls who, in their heyday, put your call through an amazing excess of wires, plugs and flashing lights on their switchboards. After the Second World War unions became much more powerful and in the 1950s and '60s a series of damaging strikes rocked heavy industry and the Government. The men of the shipyards, steelworks and coal industry began to flex their muscles with large wage claims which were stiffly resisted by employers. Both the strikes and the high wage settlements hampered the competitiveness of heavy industry, and as orders for ships dried up and coal and steel was bought cheaper from other countries, heavy industry went into a steep decline. Shipyards were eventually closed, steelworks shut down and miners found themselves retraining in other skills. But retrain many did and they also showed an enterprise that was lacking in their previous employment as small business mushroomed throughout the region. We may have lost many of the old skills, but one thing we will never lose is the enterprise of the North East worker.

Durban, South Africa, 1963. A 103-ton transformer, built at C.A. Parsons' Heaton works, is unloaded at Durban Harbour, where it will be stored until the arrival of a second unit. The transformers were for the Electricity Supply Commission of Natal and were to be used at a sub-station near Durban.

Opposite page: C.A. Parsons, Heaton, 15 January 1935. At the end of a long shift these C.A. Parsons workers found out, via the *Evening Chronicle*, that the firm had just gained a share of a lucrative £420,000 contract for a power house in Western Australia.

Simonside Terrace, 1901. This is the first tramcar from Heaton Road terminus. The driver in the picture is Titus Craggs, of Heaton.

Wingrove Depot, 1916. A clutch of clippies (and a few drivers), line up for their picture over the depot's tramlines. The second clippie from the left in the middle row is Mrs Jean Taylor, of Fenham. Jean recalled that the fare from Brighton Grove to Condercum Road was a halfpenny. The expensive-looking boots worn by the girls were issued by the company as standard.

Tyneside, 1914–18. Clippies who worked the trams on Tyneside during the First World War.

The Lord Mayor of Newcastle, Alderman T. McCutcheon, seen with a group of employees of North Coachbuilders Ltd in 1948, after he had accepted, on behalf of the corporation, the first of a fleet of seventy-seater trolleybuses to be used on the Benton circular route.

Left: Byker, 1950. Wheelwright Ron Green, aged fifty-five, cleans out the wheel hub in readiness for putting in the spokes.

Below: Ron's brother, Albert, holds the steel tyre as Ron welds the ends together.

Ron is fitting on the 'felloes' round the spokes as the wheel nears completion.

The end result as the two brothers fit the completed wheel to a cart.

Left: A Tyneside postman from the 1850s, in his distinctive uniform and horn, which may have been to warn residents of his intending delivery, because there would have been no letterboxes available at the time.

Below: Firemen from Headlam Street Station in the East End of Newcastle, *c.* 1922.

Opposite above: Jesmond, 1954. The manually operated switchboard at the Jesmond Telephone Exchange, shortly before it was replaced by the new, fully automatic exchange.

Opposite below: Heaton, 1952. Girls singing while wrapping bottles at the Lucozade factory.

Above and below: Maling pottery factory, 1930. Girls smooth off the rough parts after the various shapes leave the moulds.

Maling pottery factory, 1935. Girls at work on cups and teapots for the Royal Silver Jubilee of King George V and Queen Mary.

1936. Girls at Maling work on pottery for the forthcoming Coronation of King George VI.

Above: Maling factory, 1930. Girls carry out the craft for which they are famous for: hand-painting.

Right: Maling factory, 1950s. Girls from the Maling factory pose for the camera.

five

Heaton

The name Heaton means High Settlement, probably referring to its position above the River Ouseburn, a tributary of the River Tyne. Heaton first appears as Hactona in 1157 and then as Hoton in 1279. Hoton is also referred to as Haugh-ton, meaning the village on the Haugh of the Ouseburn. The township was included in the municipal boundaries of Newcastle in 1896. The manor of Heaton was originally part of the barony of Robert de Gaugy, who was one of King John's most trustworthy knights and who on a number of occasions entertained the king when he was in the North. Later, it belonged to the Babbingtons of Harnham. Henry Babbington was knighted by King James I for the loyal entertainment he had provided for the monarch at Heaton Hall on 1 May 1617. The Hall was eventually passed on to the Lawson family who later sold it to the Ridleys. Richard Ridley, an alderman and Mayor of Newcastle, had Heaton Hall rebuilt in 1713. The Hall was a convenient home for the family as it was situated amongst the collieries they owned. Sir Matthew White Ridley added two towers to the original Hall, which had been just a plain, square, brick building. The Hall and grounds were bought by Addison Langhorn Potter in 1840. He was so upset at its rundown condition that he immediately set about a restoration programme. He also renovated the remains of the thirteenth-century chapel known as King John's Tower. The Hall was eventually demolished in 1933 to make way for new housing, which became known as Heaton Hall Estate. Heaton Road was a major access route leading from Shields Road to the new Coast Road. From 1880 to 1910 this road, along with the many terraces, avenues and places, became a popular residential area. Tramlines were laid along Heaton Road and Shields Road in 1901, which gives an indication just how important these routes had become. For many years coal mining was an important part of Heaton's industrial heritage. On 30 April 1850 disaster struck High Heaton Colliery, which was in an area now known as Spinney Park. When miners broke through to old mine workings, water flooded the pit. Of the seventy-five miners who perished, thirty-four were mere boys. Seventy-five trees were planted on the site, one for each man and boy killed.

Opposite above: The People's Theatre, Heaton, 1962. Last-minute work goes on before the theatre opens as the Arts Centre.

Opposite below: The People's Theatre, 1963. The director coaches the actors and actresses through the final rehearsals for the play *Columbe*.

Above: Old Heaton, 1921. This picture shows a charming bit of old Heaton now long gone. This area is now the North Heaton Estate, just off Newton Road.

Right: In 1951 you were apparently breaking the law if you stood on a window sill for the purpose of cleaning or painting your window, unless the windows were those of a basement. Try telling that to this window cleaner.

Opposite, above and below: Eversley Place, 1951. Members of the Newcastle branch of Master Window Cleaners turn up for work to help out a sick colleague.

Benton Road/Coast Road, 1957. A seemingly tranquil scene at what will be a very busy road junction later in the day.

Benfield Road/Red Hall Drive, 1955. Council workmen paint the new white lines on the road at an accident blackspot. They also painted a 'slow' sign on the road at the junction which had seen more than sixty accidents in two years.

Seventh Avenue in the 1950s. We complain about the number of advertisements on the television or in newspapers today, but take a look at this shop in Heaton – at least they have left enough room for the door!

Heaton Road, 1949. It was confusion for commuters on 17 January 1949, as trolleybuses changed their numbers to coincide with new routes.

Somewhere in Northumberland, 1940. It's all smiles from these evacuees from Heaton. This class is setting out for the woods and a nature study class.

Armstrong Park, 1930. That's going down well – children enjoy a refreshing drink of water from 'Ye Well of King John' in the park. In fact it was believed to be originally a cattle trough 'for the beasts to drink from' on the farm which once incorporated the park. Why the words were carved above the well no one knows.

Above: Heaton Hall, 1928. The Hall was built overlooking the River Ouseburn. On the site there was a medieval building, traces of which were still a part of the structure when this picture was taken. The Hall was demolished in 1933. King Edward I attended the chapel in 1290 to hear a boy bishop perform the Vespers of St Nicholas, probably in connection with one of the church spectacles or plays. Later, King John paid a visit to the Hall when owned by Robert de Gaugy. The Babbingtons of Harnham occupied it afterwards and entertained King James I. The next owners of the Hall were the ancestors of Lord Ridley of Blagdon, and in 1713 Richard Ridley rebuilt the Hall. When the first Sir Matthew White Ridley came into possession he added the two towers seen above. In about 1840 the Ridleys left for Blagdon, and the estate was sold to Addison Langhorne Potter, who had started his working career as a fitter with W.G. Armstrong, but eventually had worked his way up to become a director in the company. The Hall was later owned by his grandson, Charles Potter. Some of the land had been sold off in the 1890s for the creation of Armstrong Park. The Ridleys are still at Blagdon and in the grounds stands a circular temple brought from Heaton Hall.

Right: A side-on view of Heaton Hall in 1927.

Heaton Park, 1937. Schoolchildren stroll by the bowling green in Heaton Park.

Above: Heaton Park. An oil painting of the park completed shortly after it opened in 1884.

Opposite: Heaton Park, 1952. The wide open spaces of the park are ideal for children's games.

Left: Heaton Park, 1981. A fairytale picture of the park, taken on what was said to be a glorious day.

Below: Armstrong Park, 1933. The old guns which were once on station in the park. The Parks Committee, no doubt looking at the cost of the upkeep of the guns, asked the military authorities to have them removed. The guns had been loaned to the City of Newcastle around 1900 by the Ordnance Depot.

Heaton Park, 1931. King John's Palace, or Chapel, was, according to the official rolls of Henry III in 1267, the home of Baron Adam de Gesemuth (Jesmond). He was High Sheriff of Northumberland for four years. Because of his shenanigans he got the name of an extortionist who became rich through taking the property of others. He, however, found it necessary to fortify the place for his own protection due to his behaviour. Their was great joy in the area when he failed to come home from the seventh and last Crusade in 1270.

Heaton Park, 1946. Another terrace in the park, standing above a popular vale.

Heaton Park, 1952. Gardener W. Riley tends one of the red, white and blue Coronation beds of begonias, alyssum and lobelia.

Rice

SOUP WILL BE
SUPPLIED FREE

Meat Pies
Meat Puddings
Potatoes
Peas or Beans

six

Byker

The name Byker is probably derived from 'by kiarr', meaning near a marsh. The township is bounded by Walker on the east and the Tyne on the south. Most of the northern boundary is shared with Heaton but in the north-west it touches Jesmond, very different from earlier days when Jesmond may have extended down to the River Tyne. Until 1299 Pandon Burn separated Byker and Newcastle, but it was in that year that the Borough of Newcastle was extended eastwards to a little burn called the Swirle. The land had been held by Robert of Byker and Laderena (or Ladryana), his wife, the heiress of Byker. They granted it to the king who, in turn, passed it on to the burgesses of Newcastle. In 1549 the boundaries of Newcastle were extended by an Act of Parliament at the expense of Byker, so that the ballast shore might be within the borough. Since it first started to develop, in 1865, this part of the city had undergone constant change over the ensuing years. In its early days Byker was just a small village on a hill, overlooking the river. Much later it became a series of long terraced streets on a great slope overlooking the Tyne and its magnificent bridges. Starting in 1971 Byker marked the final phase of Newcastle City Council's massive slum-clearance scheme which was finally completed in 1983. Today Byker is famous (or infamous, depending on your point of view) for the Byker Wall, a housing complex designed by architect Ralph Erskine, built in the 1960s and subject to much controversy over its aesthetic qualities.

Byker High Street, 1982. The adverts show goods, not films, as this former picture house has been converted into a superstore.

Byker tram sheds, 1904. Trams are given a fresh coat of paint and signs are painted on.

Byker car sheds, 1919. A Sentinel steam bus, belonging to Newcastle Corporation, is made ready for the Burradon and Lane Ends route.

Left: Byker Bridge, 1958. Photographer Peter Thompson catches the atmosphere of life living beneath the bridges of Byker before the days of smoke control.

Below: Byker Bridge, 1950. An audience of schoolboys watch workmen erecting scaffolding on part of the railway bridge, which was built in 1869 and needed strengthening. A work and audience situation which would never be allowed in these safety-conscious days.

Still recovering from the shock of the Byker Wall, which now stretches across the hillside where formerly streets of back-to-back houses clung tenuously to the steep slopes, the residents of Byker's old warm-hearted community were, in 1978, witnessing the emergence of the Metro flyover, a snake-like shape carefully picking its way through the remains of the old township. From the Metro station it makes its way down the side of the 'Wall', strides boldly over Shields Road and, not far from the site of the old Grand Theatre, begins its leap across the Ouseburn valley between the road bridge and the cast-iron rail bridge.

Right: Byker Bridge, *c.* 1869. The rail bridge over the Ouseburn valley soon after its completion.

Shields Road. The Meadow Dairy Company's shop with staff in the days when butter was 1s 2d a pound.

Shields Road, 1980. Well away from the heart of Newcastle, Byker's Shields Road proves an attractive shopping centre for local residents.

Shields Road, 1969. A policeman shepherds shoppers across the road while a new traffic scheme was about to be introduced to relieve congestion on the busy main street.

Salisbury Street, 1960. Children enjoy playing on the kerbside while a lorry trundles down the cobbled street which is strewn with bricks. The streets were still lit by gas lamps at night.

Commercial Road/Raby Street, 1980. Council workmen start tearing down the final properties in a slum-clearance programme which had been going on for twenty years. Since the early 1960s about 6,000 homes had been knocked down, plus shops, pubs, warehouses, garages, three schools, Headlam Street police station and the local fire station.

St Ann's Street, 1954. A beautiful but strange-looking chimney takes centre stage of this street of factories. The lone girl on the right shows that factories and housing were side by side.

Cut Bank, 1957. The view over the Ouseburn Bridge which was said to be dangerous because of heavy loads crossing throughout the day. The Council announced their intention to rebuild it.

Ringtons factory, *c.* 1930. For many years the traditional way for delivering Ringtons tea was by horse and cart.

A proud driver stands beside what could have been one of the original Ringtons horse and carts.

Central Station, 1960. Ringtons workers and their families get their train tickets checked before going on a work's outing to Scarborough.

This 1928 picture shows that vans are now working side-by-side with the Ringtons horse and carts.

SOUP WILL BE SUPPLIED FREE

Meat Pies 2 2
Meat Puddings 2 1
Potatoes 1
Peas or Beans 1

A Salvation Army motor kitchen visits Byker in 1931. With Byker being one of Tyneside's many depressed areas, the kitchen was a welcome sight, providing substantial meals at very low cost.

Residents in Byker celebrate the end of the First World War in 1918.

Byker Parish Hall, 1940. Children enjoy a Sunday school lesson during the early days of the Second World War.

The Byker Imperial Juvenile Jazz Band line up smartly to have their picture taken. Their achievements are evident by the number of trophies on display.

Above and below: Domestos factory, Albion Row, 1962. Firemen battle in vain to save the Domestos warehouse which was completely destroyed by fire. Directors of the company said that although the factory held chemicals, perfumes, packing materials and bottles, which had all been destroyed, production would not be affected. During the height of the blaze people living near the works were evacuated and a telegraph pole went up in flames and melted the overhead wires.

seven

At School

Longbenton National School, 1902. These smart youngsters must have been the apple of their teacher's eye when they won the accolade for never having been absent from class.

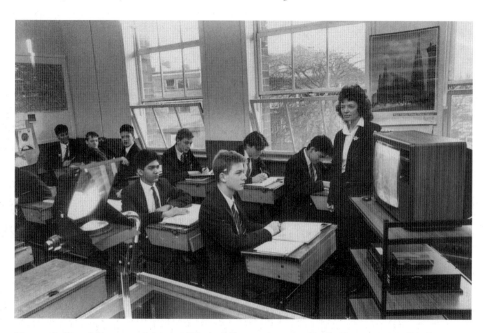

Newcastle Royal Grammar School, 1989. As full entry into the Single European Market draws nearer, languages are becoming increasingly important for every future business or professional person – teacher Mrs Pat Sainsbury takes the children through their lesson.

Above and below: 1976. Police were called in to break up a pupil strike at Heaton School in Newcastle when 200 teenage girls staged a women's lib demonstration. The girls had been protesting against a decision by teachers to use corporal punishment against them. After chanting for about an hour, the girls ran round the school and tried to get the boys to join them in their protest by shouting 'Howay the lads' – but the boys stayed at their desks. The girls then disrupted a school football match by pinching the ball.

Central High School, Jesmond, 1961. The £50,000 extension that had been opened by Sir William Cash in the same year, providing much-needed space for the 460 girls.

Chillingham Road School, 1971.

Newcastle Royal Grammar School, 1962. Tradition states that the school was founded in 1545. It was first situated at St Nicholas' Cathedral, since then it moved five times until it arrived at its present site in Jesmond which it has occupied since 1906.

Akhurst Preparatory School, 1972. Twenty-three-roomed Jesmond Cottage was built in 1831 after the style of the Newcastle architect Dobson. The stonework is so fine it is still impossible to fit a piece of paper between the blocks.

Church High, Jesmond, 1913. In the Sixth Form are, from left to right, back row: G. Rowden, M. Wills, N. Dogherty, H. Clarke, D. Morpeth, M. Davias. Middle row: M. Stenhouse, A. Young, S. Proctor, A. Inskip, U. Wilkinson, M. Sinclair, H. Cooper. Front row: L. Robson, M. Cook, I. Smith, D. Hamer, Miss Gupney, K. Bookey, G. Hodgson, G. Pestle. Foreground: D. Haydock, D. Blair.

A class from North Heaton Infant School around 1920.

Heaton, 1967. Staff at this Heaton school are determined to prevent past traditions, such as netball, being swept aside in the new comprehensive system.

Newcastle Preparatory School, 1962. Most schools usually have far more to show from an association with their old boys than mere goodwill. Confident in this knowledge, Newcastle Preparatory School launched an appeal in 1962 to all its well-wishers for financial help towards the school's modernisation and extension.

Heaton Grammar School. An archway approach gives an air of cloistered dignity to the school's quadrangle.

eight

The Ouseburn

They say everything comes around in circles. Once the Ouseburn river would have been a favourite habitat of wildlife but, as industry flourished on Tyneside the river became the lifeblood of the area. Once barges and boats scurried back and forth transferring goods from warehouse to wharves and back again. The Ouseburn also once supplied the power to drive great waterwheels and the water for certain manufacturing processes. There have been a number of potteries on Tyneside, starting with the establishment of a pottery at Pandon Dean, just west of the Ouseburn, in about 1730. It was the pottery of John Warburton which produced Brownware. By 1827 there were twenty potteries on the Tyne and most of these were in the Ouseburn area. Flint and clay came as ballast in the colliers arriving from the south and taking back coal from the Tyne. But it was a competitive business and by the 1860s, while many of the smaller potteries had ceased to function, the larger ones, such as Maling, greatly expanded their businesses. The Victoria Tunnel, a two-mile-long underground waggonway beneath the city designed to carry coal from a colliery at Spital Tongues, and which emerged at Ouseburn, is one of the famous relics of the past. The Ouse Street entrance is one of the few remaining access points into this historic structure. It opened in 1842 but the colliery closed in 1857, making the tunnel redundant. At its deepest it was 85ft below the ground and 6-7ft 8in high by 6ft 3in wide. During the Second World War it was also used as an air-raid shelter. Today the Ouseburn is of no importance to industry and has returned as a habitat for wildlife once again as well as being developed as a leisure area.

Salter's Bridge, 1933. Classed as an ancient monument, it straddles the Ouseburn.

Jesmond Vale, 1944. The Ouseburn flows through the Vale. In the background is Armstrong Bridge.

'Operation Clean-up', 1971. Volunteers use a small boat to collect rubbish from the Ouseburn.

Danger, 1955. An open sewer deposits its filth into the Ouseburn in an area where children play, close to Benton Bank.

The construction of the culvert over the Ouseburn in 1906. During the Second World War the culvert was used as an air-raid shelter by local residents.

Left: Ouseburn Valley, 1860. A picture taken when it was said there was more burn than ouse.

Below: Ouseburn Reclamation, 1969. Once a well-used – but unauthorised – tipping site, it was decided to plant trees and make the land available for leisure use.

Above: Ouseburn Tip, 1929. It was hoped that one of Newcastle's black spots could be turned into a beauty spot. Eventually, the City Stadium was built on the site, as the picture on the right shows.

Right: The first stage of the City Stadium nearing its completion in 1954. Workers are putting the edging in place for the cinder running track, the middle is almost ready for seeding to provide the soccer pitch.

Byker Bridge, 1969. A bus passes over the bridge, and businesses and derelict factories line the Ouseburn below.

Opposite, above and below: Ouseburn Valley, 1973. The land reclamation is now well underway. Gone are the ugly heaps of rubbish and the wrecks of abandoned cars *(opposite below)*. The area has become known as the Ouseburn Park. Tin cans and broken bottles have given way to trees and benches. Crawford Bridge, seen in the centre of the picture *(opposite above)*, spanning the Ouseburn, is the oldest bridge in the city and has been repaved with cobbles from the streets of Byker and the grass has been mown and interspersed with shrubs.

Above and left: Newcastle Motorboat Club, above 1970 and below, 1966. A peaceful haven surrounded by scrapyards and factories. Amidst these unlikely surroundings lies a selection of fascinating small boats. The boats are used mainly for holidays and fishing.

nine

People

Walker Naval Yard, 1930. The yard was besieged by men anxious for work. Some hoped to get a start on a new liner to be constructed there.

Longbenton, 1951. Crowds gather to watch the opening of the Royal Artillery houses at Longbenton by General Sir Alan Cunningham.

Above: Gibson Street washhouse. In 1948, above, it was said that washing clothes need not be a solitary servitude. Apparently more use was being made of the premises than ten years earlier and the system saved money, fuel and made better-tempered husbands.

Left: 1968. Steam was rising and tempers running high as the Council had made a decision to close the Gibson Street washhouse at the end of that financial year. One user complained that she washed for a family of seven: 'We don't have room for a big washer in our flat'.

Willington Athletic, pre-1914. The club ceased to exist after the outbreak of the First World War.

Heaton Park. Hopefully the starter has a blank in his pistol as he seems to be pointing it at the man on his right as he is about to start a race

The Newcastle Tramways Band, smartly turned out to have their picture taken in 1911.

Letch Cottage. In 1894 a plot of land was bought in the Willow Dene area of Forest Hall and a very desirable cottage was built for the bearded gentleman and his family. He also had adjoining stables built for the horses in the picture.

City Road, 1968. Policemen keep watch as technicians from Tyne Tees Television demonstrate outside the studios over a dispute with the management.

Parsons workers, 1970. Members of DATA from the firm of C.A. Parsons marching to a strike meeting in Newcastle.

Longbenton DSS, 1975. The great race is on as the workers head for home at the end of a long day at the office.

Central High School, Jesmond, 1979. Girls from the choir are ready to represent the North East in the finals of a national competition on London Weekend Television's South Bank Show. Before they left Newcastle they were presented with a lucky mascot, Candy the giant panda.

Above and right: New Bridge Street, 1959. Fire-fighters finally bring under control a blaze which has destroyed a huge five-storey Newcastle warehouse. At the height of the fire a crowd of 20,000 watched as flames surged through the building, with the roof caving in and floors giving way. Traffic was halted as flames leapt across the road threatening other buildings and at the rear of the building trains were re-routed as the fire spread to Manors Station. The building housed firms such as Hotpoint, Tyres (Scotland) Ltd, Philips Electrical Ltd, the New Bridge post office, the Weslyan General District Assurance office and Summerfield Ltd, wholesale distributors. Luckily no one was hurt in the blaze.

Walkergate telephone depot, 1973. When customers' calls swamp the switchboard, a system of lights, seen under the wall clock, show the operators the number of calls awaiting attention.

Street trading, 1938. This East End street trader found times so hard that he had to, on occasions, pawn his barrow to raise some cash.

Other local titles published by Tempus

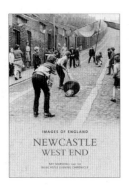

Newcastle West End

RAY MARSHALL AND THE NEWCASTLE EVENING CHRONICLE

This superb collection of photographs from the *Newcastle Evening Chronicle*'s picture library gives an insight into people's lives and the changes they experienced in the West End of Newcastle during the last century. It remembers the great 1960s and '70s clearances and charts the rapid growth of Elswick, Scotswood, Fenham and Benwell. This book will help people recall their fond — if hard — past.

0-7524-3351-2

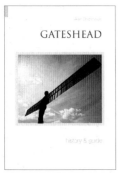

Gateshead History and Guide

ALAN BRAZENDALE

This book describes Gateshead's history from Roman settlements, through its industrial days when Dr Johnson unflatteringly described it as 'a dirty lane leading to Newcastle', to the modern Gateshead, famous for its International Stadium, Angel of the North, and Baltic Centre for Contemporary Art. This is an honest portrayal written from the heart of one of Gateshead's loyal citizens, who is not only a local historian but also a former Mayor of Gateshead.

0-7524-3207-9

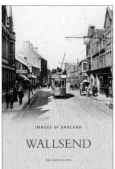

Wallsend

KEN HUTCHINSON

This collection of over 200 photographs of Wallsend has been assembled from the archives of Wallsend Local History Society and North Tyneside Libraries. It illustrates some of the many changes and developments that have taken place in the town over the last hundred years. The photographs recall a time when the riverside was still dominated by shipbuilding and coal mining was a major local employer. With images of long-lost shops and businesses, cinemas and schools, this book is a nostalgic and heart-warming journey into the recent past.

0-7524-3424-1

Jarrow

PAUL PERRY

Jarrow was once a sparsely populated area which swelled to a population of 40,000 when industry boomed in the 1920s. Around ten years later, Jarrow faced decline. Using a fascinating collection of over 200 images, this book shows the rise, unexpected fall and further rise of Jarrow. Professional photographer Paul Perry also compiled *Jarrow Then & Now*, a pictorial history charting the changing face of the town and its skyline.

0-7524-3336-9

If you are interested in purchasing other books published by Tempus, or in case you have difficulty finding any Tempus books in your local bookshop, you can also place orders directly through our website

www.tempus-publishing.com